Let's Talk About
FEELING INFERIOR

AN INTERPERSONAL FEELINGS BOOK

Written by Joy Berry   Illustrated by Roey

Hello, my name is Belle.
I'd like to tell you a story
about my friend, Katie.

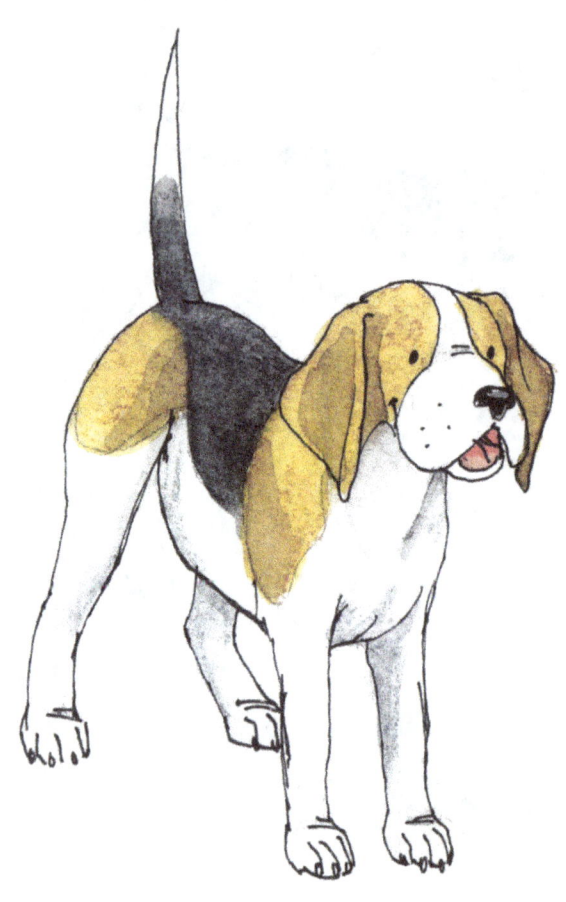

Some people know information that Katie does not know. Sometimes Katie feels that these people are better than she is. Katie feels inferior.

Sometimes Katie thinks that other people are better looking than she is.
Katie feels that these people are better than she is.
Katie feels inferior.

She is better than I am because she _is_ prettier than I am.

Some people have things that Katie does not have.
Sometimes Katie feels that these people are better than she is.
Katie feels inferior.

When you feel inferior, you feel as though you are not as valuable or as important as another person.

Feeling inferior can cause you to doubt whether or not you can do something. When you doubt whether or not you can do something, you might not try to do it. You will not be able to do something that you do not try to do.

So, feeling inferior can keep you from doing the things that you want or need to do.

I wouldn't even try to do that because I know I couldn't do it.

Try not to feel inferior around people who know information that you do not know. Remember these things:
- Knowing information does not make a person better than anyone else.
- No one can know everything there is to know.
- Everyone is smart in his or her own way.

To avoid feeling inferior around people who know information that you do not know, do these things:
- Think about all of the things you <u>do</u> know.
- Be proud of what you know.
- Realize that you have the ability to learn and to know more.
- Do whatever you can to learn new information.

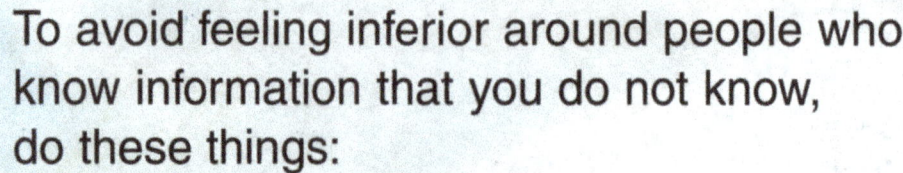

Try not to feel inferior around people who can do things that you cannot do. Remember these things:
- Being able to do something does not make a person better than anyone else.
- No one can do everything.
- Everyone can do something well.

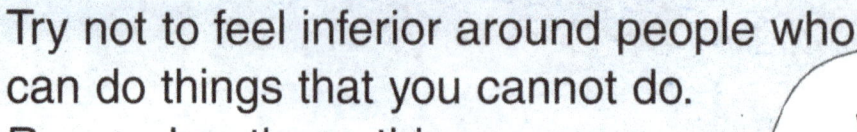

Wow! That looks <u>hard</u> to do. Do you think I could learn how to do it?

To avoid feeling inferior around people who
can do things that you can not do,
do these things:
- Think about all of the things that you <u>can</u> do.
- Be proud of what you can do.
- Realize that you have the ability to learn how to do new things.
- Do whatever you can to learn how to do new things.

Try not to feel inferior around people who you think are better looking than you are. Remember these things:
- The way a person looks is only a small part of what makes the person beautiful.
- A person's beauty is also determined by how the person acts.
- A person who is respectful and kind is beautiful.
- A person who is disrespectful and rude is not very beautiful.

To avoid feeling inferior around people who you think are better looking than you are, do these things:
- Become a beautiful person by being respectful and kind.
- Realize that keeping yourself clean can add to your beauty.
- Wear neat and clean clothes that will help you to look good and to feel good about yourself.

Try not to feel inferior around people who have things that you do not have. Remember these things:
- A person's possessions have nothing to do with whether or not the person is important.
- Everyone is important.
- No one is more important than anyone else.
- Everyone is important in his or her own way.

To avoid feeling inferior around people who have things that you do not have,
do these things:
- Realize that no one has everything he or she wants.
- Realize that you can not have everything that you want.
- Think about all of the things that you <u>do</u> have.
- Be thankful for the things that you have.

Remember that everyone feels inferior at one time or another. So, do not feel ashamed about feeling inferior. Instead, whenever you are feeling inferior, do things that will make you feel better about yourself.

What do you do when you feel inferior?

CREDITS

Senior Editor ....Marilyn Berry

Managing Editor ....Keith D. Stewart

Project Manager ....Jim Wools

Print Production Manager ....Joe Cudmore

Copy Editor ....Tom McIntyre

Electronic Production ....Tonia Farnell, Grace Guerra-Milke
Marty Osckel, Dan Dever

Editorial Consultants ....Lisa Berry, Carol Sauder, Mel Sauder

Copyright © Joy Berry, 2022
Originally Published, 1986

All rights are reserved.

No part of this book can be duplicated or used without the prior written permission of the copyright owner, except for the use of brief quotations from the book.

For inquiries or permission requests contact the publisher.

Published by Joy Berry Enterprises
www.joyberryenterprises.com

www.ingramcontent.com/pod-product-compliance
Lightning Source LLC
Chambersburg PA
CBHW081412070526
44583CB00020B/2772